Old Clarkston and Nethe...

by Douglas Nisbet

The heart of old Netherlee on Clarkston Road, including Prosser's newsagent shop. Children who lived in these tenements attended Netherlee Primary School. One of the school's first pupils, Bobby Wood, now living in East Kilbride, was born in the tenements in 1928. His parents married in the Mission Hall which was down Burnside Road near Netherlee Mill, and his grandparents lived in the old mill houses. The tenements were demolished in the mid-1930s and replaced with McLaren Place, which was named after the last occupant of Netherlee House who owned the land. Completed just before the Second World War, only half the shops were occupied until 1945. Mr Jaconelli Snr of the Derby Café was one of the first occupants. At that time Netherlee had five grocers – Mitchell, Galbraith, Barclay, Cochrane and the Co-op – and now there are none.

© Douglas Nisbet, 2007
First published in the United Kingdom, 2007,
by Stenlake Publishing Ltd.
www.stenlake.co.uk
ISBN 9781840333893
Printed by Blissetts, Roslin Road, Acton, W3 8DH

A Rover, registration number HS 5903, with its owner James Nisbet and two of his three sons, Douglas and John. Purchasing the car in 1930, James had never driven before but was confident that as the Rover dealer, Mr Gibbons, had taken him out to Eaglesham to see the car, he would instantly be able to drive back! Fortunately, the roads were reasonably quiet. The car was only taken out of the garage on Saturdays, for a 'run' to the Clyde Coast or the lochs. Bought brand new, it cost £255 and had a two-year guarantee. The starting handle was at the front, the battery was on the side step and the spare tyre was attached to the rear luggage rack. With no heater in winter, passengers had to wear heavy coats, gloves, scarves, muffs, thick rugs and even foot muffs. The car had no seat belts and sometimes humpback bridges would cause the passengers to hit the inside of the roof, on one occasion smashing the roof light. In those days, all the AA and RAC patrolmen saluted when passing and provided a most efficient breakdown service. Holidays were definitely an adventure in those days: going up the 'Rest and be Thankful' with the radiator steaming, and requiring a rest and some rocking to reach the top; or sailing to Arran, when the driver had to negotiate two planks between the pier and the boat, and then park between the funnels.

Further Reading

The books listed below were used by the author during his research. None are available from Stenlake Publishing. Those interested in finding out more are advised to contact their local bookshop or reference library.

Eastwood District Libraries, *A History of Clarkston* (1988).
Nisbet, D.S., *Old Netherlee* (1990) and *More Old Netherlee* (1992).
Nisbet, S.M., *The Four Paper Mills of Cathcart* (1998).

Nisbet, S.M., *A History of Stamperland* (1999).
Welsh, T.C., *Eastwood District, History & Heritage* (1989).

INTRODUCTION
by Stuart M. Nisbet

The area of Netherlee and Clarkston was originally known as the Lands of Lee. In the 1500s this was split into Netherlee, Midlee (latterly Stamperland) and Overlee. The modern area began to develop in the 1660s when the nearby Bogton Estate was broken up. James, the second son of Maxwell of Bogton, took the land known as the William Wood and began to develop a new estate. At its peak, Williamwood Estate included parts of Cathcart, Busby, Eastwood and Mearns parishes. Two areas remained separate - the part of Netherlee towards Muirend, which was in Aikenhead Estate, and Overlee which continued as a small private estate. Clarkston came along much later.

At the heart of James Maxwell's estate was his new mansion, Williamwood House. By coincidence this was built close to the traditional centre of the area, the fourteenth-century castle of Lee. The site of the castle was identified in the 1980s as the motte in Beechgrove Park, Netherlee. By 1700 there were only four families in the area, who lived in a hamlet or 'fermtoun' down on the banks of the River Cart, but through the ambitious plans of the Maxwells, Williamwood Estate experienced a remarkable growth. Trees were planted and the land was drained and enclosed. The population of the area began to increase and local life was dominated by the Maxwells, who held courts several times a year where local debts and differences were settled.

Along with the agricultural improvements came the development of industry and transport. The River Cart powered numerous mills in the Netherlee area. Among the earliest were waulk mills on either side of the waterfall at Linn, used for washing and softening cloth or leather. The Netherlee side of the waterfall was known as Waulkersland, after a seventeenth-century waulk mill. On the opposite side of the falls was another waulk mill, worked by the Wilkie family who are buried in Cathcart Kirkyard.

The first paper mill in the area was founded at Newlands in the 1680s by a French immigrant. In 1700 his son-in-law expanded the business with a larger paper mill at Netherlee and a hamlet began to develop around this. In 1730 the paper mill moved down to Millholm and Netherlee Waulk Mill restarted. By 1749 a snuff mill was added, with four water-powered machines for grinding snuff. In 1766 a large bleachfield was also in operation for bleaching cloth and thread. Each of these contributed to the growth of Netherlee, which by the 1790s had expanded from the original riverside site to the area of the present centre at McLaren Place.

Netherlee Paper Mill started up again in 1771 and the owner, John Muir, built Netherlee Mansion House above the mill. A string of mill owners occupied it, including Archibald McGown who worked the paper mill until 1834. The site then became a calico printworks, used to bleach, print and dye cotton cloth. Employment fluctuated between 200 and 400 until the 1880s, most living at Netherlee and Clarkston. The vagaries of the calico printing trade meant that, due to downturns in trade, hundreds were regularly thrown out of work and forced to move to other areas. A substantial number of Netherlee's children were born at Bonhill Printworks on the River Leven, as the workforce moved back and forth to keep employment. The paper mill was later used as a laundry, with the buildings, chimneys and dam surviving until the 1940s and the tunnelled lades until the 1960s, when they were crushed by bulldozers.

The river valley was also the location of coal and limestone mining all the way from Cathcart to Overlee. This increased greatly from the 1750s and by the 1790s Williamwood Colliery had a large steam-pumping engine and its own short-lived mining settlement at Mavisbank. Advances in agriculture relied on lime to improve the soil and the mining of coal to burn the limestone. Lime working became the main employer in the parish in the 1790s and there were various quarries and mines including those at Bogton, Linn and Overlee. This industry continued into the 1860s with larger quarries and kilns in the area of Williamwood golf course producing limestone cement, bricks and tiles. The products were taken out to Eastwoodmains Road at Drumby Farm by a tramway. When the railway to Busby arrived, a special bridge was built taking the wagons under the railway. This bridge, behind the current Drumby Crescent, was later used for access from Radleigh House to the golf club but is now disused.

Sandstone quarrying was also a large industry, with Williamwood Quarry extending east from the better-known Giffnock and Braidbar quarries. The Neilston railway was built through Williamwood Quarry, although part of it survived into the 1940s and is remembered as a very deep and flooded hole. Other mysterious mounds and holes along the river remain as a reminder of the area's industrial past.

Although the Netherlee area was originally sparsely populated, it was never a backwater as the old road from Glasgow to Kilmarnock passed though its centre. Roadways in Scotland were greatly improved from the late 1780s, and a road was built from Paisley to East Kilbride via a new bridge over the Cart at Busby. Clarkston was in many ways a branch of Netherlee, as it grew due to the jobs available in the water-powered industries at Netherlee and also at Busby. The name 'Clarkston' first appeared in the 1790s, at the junction of the Old Mearns Road with the new road from Paisley to East Kilbride. A man by the name of Clark built a house and stables at the toll point and Clarkston began. The closure of side roads forced traffic to pass through the toll points; the old road from Cathcart to Netherlee via a ford at Linn was forcibly closed in the 1790s and Slamanshill Road (now Stamperland Avenue) was closed to all but farm traffic in 1848.

Clarkston Toll was situated on the corner of the four farms of Slamanshill, Overlee, Carolside and Drumby and in 1801 was advertised by the Maxwells as a site for a new village. However, decades passed before it grew significantly. By the 1850s Clarkston was populated mainly by calico printers who worked at Netherlee, but was still just a small number of houses clustered around the toll.

In the 1860s a railway through Clarkston to Busby Printworks was opened. The railway also benefited Netherlee Printworks, which purchased a large chunk of land at Clarkston Toll for their railway siding (on the site of the car park at Clarkston Hall). Again Netherlee's influence boosted Clarkston's population. Other railways planned at the same time would have carved up the area even more. A proposed railway from Cathcart through Netherlee to Kilmarnock was started but then abandoned. Another line was planned to Netherlee Printworks and carrying on to Carmunnock. This was designed to soar across Netherlee village on a huge viaduct, totally changing the area, but this was also never built.

House building in the area relied on the release of land by the dwindling estates. Part of the Aikenhead Estate was sold for the building of the Ormondes at Netherlee and for Linn Park around the First World War. Williamwood Golf Club was founded in 1906 and its course competed with housing for green space. In the 1920s the last Stewart of Williamwood died and the estate was carved up between several builders, including Andrew Mitchell. The arrival of trams to and from Glasgow city centre in 1921 was as influential as the railway and encouraged further building. The building boom accelerated in the 1930s with construction of the bungalows at Netherlee and Clarkston. These growing communities required education facilities and the private Arundel School was established in the early twentieth century. The first public schools were Netherlee Primary, built in 1932, and Eastwood (later Williamwood) Secondary in 1937. Meanwhile, the first church between Clarkston and Netherlee started as a mission hall beside the River Cart around 1900. The congregation expanded and built Netherlee Church in 1933. Housing filled the gap between Netherlee and Clarkston – the area known as Stamperland - and its church was opened in the 1940s with the synagogue following in the 1950s.

The farm steadings outlasted their fields. Netherlee Farm disappeared to housing from the 1930s, Stamperland in the mid 1930s, and Carolside lasted into the 1960s. Overlee farmhouse, dating from the early 1800s, still survives as one of the oldest buildings in the area. As each farm and field was sold off to the builders the modern area spread, but despite all the changes over the last 300 years the locations of the old farms and fields can still be identified - with a little imagination!

Acknowledgements

The author wishes to thank the following for their assistance while he was preparing this book: Stuart M. Nisbet, Ken A.C. Melvin, Mrs Jane Borland, Mrs Jess Whyte, Mrs Elizabeth Stewart, Amanda Robb of Giffnock Library, Maureen Craig, Robert C. Wood and Netherlee Church of Scotland.

Picture Acknowledgements

The publishers wish to thank the following for contributing photographs to this book:
East Renfrewshire Council for pages 1, 11, 20 (copyright Richard Orr), 25, 26, 29, 38, 40, 41 (copyright Paul McNamara), 42, 44 (copyright Paul McNamara), 46, inside back cover, Jess Whyte for pages 14 and 15; Andrew Eadie for page 19; Betty Turner for page 22; the late Ken A.C. Melvin for page 32; Stuart Nisbet for the map and pages 5, 9 and 33; and Douglas Nisbet for pages 2, 8,16,17 and 37

In 1933 the Toledo Cinema was designed, with a Spanish theme, by the architect William Beresford Inglis. Originally seating nearly 1,600, in 1982 it was converted internally to house three cinemas. It closed in October 2001 and the B-listed façade was retained when the building was converted into flats. In the years before widespread television, the cinema was very popular with the locals, many of whom visited twice weekly, often queuing outside for the second house. A canopy was built around both sides to shelter waiting patrons from the weather. The price of entry ranged from four to twelve old pence. In the early 1960s the Saturday morning matinee, known as the 'ABC Minors', was a great attraction for local children. Hamilton's Bogton Farm and Dairy adjoined the Toledo, and the cinema was built on its pony track. On his way to Holmlea school, this writer would watch the prize high-stepping horses of the farm perform, although they usually earned their keep with the more mundane task of pulling milk carts. One of the horses was called Toledo. Locals welcomed Hamilton's mobile dairy, as it also deposited free manure at the door! The farm was replaced in the mid-1960s by a Safeway (now Somerfield), at the time one of the first American-style supermarkets in Scotland. A mansion, Bogton House, stood east of the farm, near Bute Gardens, between 1700 and 1906.

In 1928 the United Free Church of Scotland opened the hall on the left of this photograph, at the corner of Ormonde Avenue and Ormonde Drive. The noticeboard indicates that a church was to be added on the empty site in the foreground and the hall was used for worship in the six years leading up to the building of the church (it is now the church hall). The hall had a pedal organ and wooden tip-up seats which always caused a clatter at the start of each hymn. The stage provided the 'chancel', with the choir on either side of the minister.

Netherlee Church of Scotland opened next to the hall in 1934. By that time the Church of Scotland and the United Free Church had amalgamated. Of modern gothic design, it was constructed of pink sandstone from Corncockle Quarry, near Annan. The building cost £13,931, only £13 over the estimate. The interior is very bright, with light oak seating, and more than half the windows are of stained glass. In 1970 the church purchased the largest mansion in the area, Kingsley House, which stands opposite the Linn Park Gates. Initially built for Mr Gordon, who had a large warehouse in the city, it was later occupied by a Doctor Burton who was Jewish and held religious meetings there during the war. His widow helped the church purchase the house (as it required additional meeting rooms) and it was renamed Kirk House. Inside there is an oil painting by a Mr Allan (who lived in a large house in Clarkston Road opposite Parklands Road) depicting the area of the Ormondes before any housing was built.

The 278th Glasgow Company of the Boys' Brigade in 1939. Sitting directly in the centre of the first row is the 'Skipper', Len Dalziel, who founded the company in 1936. Sadly, several of those pictured here were killed in the Second World War. About a dozen still reside in the district, all now in their eighties. For the first fifty years the company met in Netherlee Primary School free of charge (it now meets in Netherlee Church hall). The early company prided itself in marching to and from all district parades, even to Croftfoot in the snow, and early summer camps were held in Gullane and Cullen.

Back row (left to right): Stanley Ferrier, Willie Hogg, Roy Taylor, Jack Dalziel, George Proud, Norman Ronald, Douglas Taylor, J. Wilson, John Nisbet, John Henderson, Bill Glendinning, Alistair Fairweather, Douglas Lambie, Eddie Millree, David Gilchrist, Cecil Trent.

Third row: Bert Warner, Jim Barbour, Martin Cruickshanks, Andrew Carson, Ronald Berry, Tom Scott, George McIntosh, Richard Armour, Tom Wright, Donald Macrae, Jimmy Dixon, John Jamieson, Harold Robertson, Robbie Stewart, Douglas Nisbet.

Second row: Peter Binnie, Cyril Main, D. Duncan, David Crawford, Ian Dick, Ronnie Warner, Robin Scott, J.O. Robertson, Robb Brown, Willie Walker, Billy Iyoob, Bill Clow, Campbell Harvey, Matt Boyd, Roy Dunn, Ian Taylor, Charlie Duncan.

First row: Reg Cruddace, Tom White, Neil Scott, R. McIlwham, W. Coventry, Bob Watson, 'Skipper' Len Dalziel, John Watson, J. McIlvride, A. Muir, Jimmy Campbell, John Jamieson, J.M. Robertson, Jim Wood.

Described in 1811 as 'a genteel house with a view of the River Cart', Linn House was built by the Gordons of Aikenhead. The house was doubled in size by the addition of the bay-windowed extension in 1852 by prominent architect Charles Wilson. It was occupied by various industrialists, including West Indies merchant 'Sugar' Campbell, the Hendersons of the shipping line, and rubber merchant 'Gutta Percha' Dick who made 'sannies' (gym shoes). In 1919 the estate was acquired by Glasgow Corporation and made into a public park. The house was latterly used as a tea room, then a museum. Abandoned and threatened with demolition by 2004, it was saved by public protest and has been converted to four residential apartments.

Built in 1835, Linn Park's Ha'penny Bridge is the oldest cast-iron bridge in Glasgow. Before it was built, the river was crossed by a ford from Linn to Netherlee just upstream, at the end of Burnside Road. The ford was forcibly closed to avoid toll evasion by travellers from Cathcart to Netherlee. The river is subject to severe winter floods, such as the one seen in this photograph from October 1990. Large trees have even been swept down and rammed into the bridge. It narrowly avoided destruction during the Second World War when a stray German bomb just missed it.

Linn Park's bandstand, where entertainers once performed several times weekly. On Sundays brass bands played and many spectators sat on the hill directly behind the seats to avoid the entry charge which could be one to three old pence! To the south of the bandstand were Linn Gardens, at one time a blaze of colour and latterly a children's zoo. Adjacent to the gardens are some surviving cottages of Linn Farm steading. These sit in woodland within former lime quarries and now incorporate a riding centre. The bandstand was demolished in the 1960s.

In summer, Sunday school trips visited the park and if it rained the groups would shelter and play games in the Park's pavilion. Sadly, for years the pavilion was left to vandals and it was finally demolished. The adjacent field still shows very prominent corrugations of 'rig and furrow', the remnants of medieval ploughing on Linn farm. Through the hedge behind the pavilion site is Linn Crematorium, built in the 1960s.

The Tower de Paris Tearooms were very popular in the 1920s and '30s. They were situated at the north end of where McLaren Place now stands, adjoining Linn Park. At weekends thousands came out from the city by tram to visit the park and tearooms. They were demolished about 1933 when the adjoining Netherlee tenements were also pulled down. This writer can remember, as a wee boy, using his Saturday penny at the Nestle's chocolate 'machine' outside the tearooms.

Diack and Lambie's Linn Park Garage was in business between 1925 and 1958. Among the services it offered were overnight lockup facilities, with each car secured in a cage. The garage stretched along behind the shops in front of Netherlee Primary School. During the Second World War it accommodated a local Auxiliary Fire Service and sixteen girls were also employed making gun parts. In later years the site became a BP filling station and, finally, modern flats.

Mr Lambie, local garage owner, watching firemen practising during the Second World War in the ruins of one of the five-storey buildings of Netherlee Printworks. This photograph is actually a frame from a film record of the event. The buildings, down beside the Cart behind Netherlee Primary School, had three tall chimneys and their final use was as a laundry before they were demolished in the 1950s. Above the mills was Netherlee House, built in the 1760s and home of a succession of millowners. The mansion house, demolished in the 1920s, was reached by a long tree-lined driveway, now Linnpark Avenue.

The football team of the 278th Company, Boys' Brigade in 1947. The team played a Saturday league along with the other Glasgow B.B. teams. At Netherlee the pitch sloped down towards the school. The bottom half tended to flood after heavy rain so that sometimes matches could only be played on the top half! The players originally used one of the old mill buildings as a changing room and later had to climb the school railings to use the playground shelters as the school gates were always locked. This photograph was taken shortly before the demolition of the Netherlee Mill, as can be seen by one of the tall chimneys in the background on the right.

Front row (left to right): Willie Hunter, Eric Stoker, Ian McKenzie, Watson Muirhead.

Back row: Ian Harris, Ron Trevorrow, Ian Hunter, Alastair Kerr, Duncan McClure, Ian Lambie, Angus Bell.

Netherlee Primary School opened in 1933 and was only one storey high due to the coal workings beneath. Nevertheless, it was informally known as the 'Sunshine School' because of its quantity of windows. In this photograph from 1936 the teacher is David Carslaw, who taught this class for all seven years of their primary education. The headmaster at that time was Mr Bannatyne, a strong disciplinarian who left a deep impression on this writer after he was caught riding on the back step of Hamilton's milk cart and given three of the belt! The main school corridor had the unusual feature of traffic lights which indicated when to leave classrooms. One memorable school outing in the 1930s was to watch the ocean liner *Queen Mary* sailing down the Clyde at Erskine.

Front row (left to right): Jimmie Milne, Bryce Robertson, John Jamieson, David Crawford, George McIntosh, Ian Smillie, Tom Scott, Kenneth Milne;
Second row: Core (first name unknown), unknown, Doreen Bone, Betty Turner, unknown, Lilias Young, Nora Buchanan, Jean Marshall, Connie (surname unknown), (first name unknown) Wallace, Doreen McIntyre.
Third row: Ian Wallace, Alex Roberston, (first name unknown) Duff, rest unknown.
Fourth row: Douglas Nisbet, Mitchell Watt, Cecil Trent, Stanley Dobbie, Tom Young, Ian Forson, Billy Iyoob, (first name unknown) Nicholson, Jimmy Dickson, unknown.
Back row: Arthur Crowe, Douglas Taylor, Tom Booth, Tom Barclay, Donald McLean, Gordon Munro, unknown, Norman Ronald, Gordon Watson.

Netherlee Farm was last operated by Ian and William Clark and closed in 1932. The site was then taken by bungalows and the shops at the start of Netherburn Avenue. The farmhouse stood beside the hillock or motte in the small park behind the post office. In 1984 the giant beech tree visible behind the farm was blown down, exposing early pottery among its roots, confirming this as the site of Lee Castle. Netherlee's farmland stretched from Nethervale Avenue down to Netherlee Primary School, including an area across Clarkston Road, where a field known as 'Williamwood Park' is now the site of the streets which take that name.

Netherlee Farm photographed from the east in 1932, showing the last harvest before the demolition of the farm. The central white buildings are the original courtyard farm. The roof of the later farmhouse (shown on the opposite page) is just visible behind, followed by the semi-detatched villas on Clarkston Road. In the foreground the roads are partly built up for the new bungalow development, with Nethercliffe Avenue in the foreground, Leefield Drive crossing the picture, and Netherburn Avenue on the top right.

An aerial photograph from 1929 looking north from Williamwood Golf Course down Clarkston Road. In the centre foreground is Beechlands House while to the left of the photograph are the semi-detached houses of the caretaker and chauffeur at Williamwood House. On the right, Netherlee Farm can be seen behind the trees. Further up Clarkston Road is Diack and Lambie's Garage, but neither Netherlee School or McLaren Place had been built at that time. Andrew Mitchell bought the grounds of the former Williamwood Home Farm and built Beechlands House and coach house in the 1920s. Mitchell also owned the land which became Williamwood Golf Course and built many of the red sandstone houses in south Netherlee, including those on First Avenue. Beechlands House was demolished around 1970 and its grounds now contain flats.

A gas-powered bus at Williamwood Lodge on Clarkston Road. The bus was owned by Halley's Industrial Motors, Yoker, who operated it on a service between Netherlee and Eaglesham. Williamwood House had two gatehouses, or 'lodges', both on Clarkston Road. The southern lodge, at the end of modern Beechlands Drive, was known as Stamperland Lodge. By 1810 the mail coach called at Stamperland Lodge everyday, and by the 1850s horse-drawn omnibuses passed the gate three times daily. The northern lodge was near the end of Williamwood Drive. The first Williamwood House was built by the Maxwells in the 1600s. In 1678 John Maxwell, the then laird, had to forfeit the estate for assisting the Covenanting cause. A Conventicle was being held on his land when Highland soldiers arrived and took 60 Covenanters prisoner. They were sentenced to transportation to the West Indies as slaves, but were given their freedom at London Docks when no vessels could convey them abroad. The Maxwells got back their estate and replaced the house with a new structure in the 1790s. One hundred years later this was itself replaced by a new house built by the Stewart family. The current Williamwood House was erected by Mitchell the builder in 1929 for George Urie Scott, the owner of the Pavilion Theatre. His widow left the house to the Church of Scotland and it is now a home for the elderly. The old orchard is now part of the first hole at Williamwood Golf Course, where traces of the orchard walls can still be seen, plus a surviving plum tree. Williamwood Golf Club was founded in 1906 and the course is situated mainly on the lands of Drumby and Muirhouse farms.

In the middle of Williamwood Golf Course stands Drumby Cottage which was originally part of Williamwood Tile Works. This extracted fireclay from extensive quarries covering the lower part of the golf course near the pond. In 1934 Betty Turner and her sister Sheila lived in one room of this cottage with their parents, as the only other room was unfit for habitation. Her father was one of the greenkeepers and the front door was seldom used, as golf balls regularly flew over the house. The cottage was lit by oil lamps and had an iron range for cooking. Two bed recesses were built against the wall. Water was collected from an old pump outside and a zinc bath was used weekly. The cottage was declared unfit for habitation in 1938 (although it is still in use as a greenkeeper's store) and the family moved to a council house in Busby.

Stamperland House and Farm, photographed here from the bottom of modern Stamperland Drive, was situated where Orchy Gardens in the centre of The Oval now stands. Demolished in 1935, the house was last occupied by Andrew Paterson of Camp Coffee fame. Stamperland House's gatehouse was the bungalow which still stands in Stamperland Gardens, in the hollow below the edge of Stamperland Hill. The farm outhouses were used by Lawrence the builder while erecting the terraced homes in Stamperland. The first houses were priced between £350 and £500 (£25 down and 15 shillings or one pound per week).

Trams to Clarkston started in 1921 and initially stopped short of the bridge over the railway. It was a relatively safe method of transport and the vehicles had cowcatchers at the front. Fares were only a few pence and were collected by a conductor or deposited in a wee red box. When the road was recently dug up at Clarkston Toll a stretch of cobbles and tram rails was exposed.

Two of the very last trolley buses to Clarkston, on Clarkston Road near First Avenue. The trolley buses operated from the end of the Clarkston tram service in 1953 until 1967. The buses had a distinctive hum from their electric motors and took power from the same overhead wires as the trams. Their trolleys often slipped off the overhead wires and the conductor had to get out and replace them using a long wooden pole stored under the bus.

A view in the early 1930s from Hillview Drive, looking down towards Williamwood railway bridges in the distance. Most of the bungalows were completed by this time and by the time the photograph was taken the terraced houses of Cleuch Gardens were under construction. However, Williamwood Church and Eastwood School had not yet been built. In 2006 housing is again being built, this time on the grassy slope in the foreground.

A view of the recently built housing development known as Carolside Park about 1930. Williamwood Golf Clubhouse is the lone building in the distance, left of centre. Stamperland Hill is in the far right, above the steep parkland, seen before Clarkston Hall and Library were built.

Suburban life in Clarkston as the Hogarth family visit the Hutcheson family at 5 Sunnyside Drive in September 1938. In the above photograph from left: Jenny Hutcheson, Graham Hogarth, Maureen Hutcheson, Doreen Hogarth, Doreen's boyfriend, Dorothy Hogarth.

This school was opened in Seres Road in 1937 and named 'Eastwood' for its first 38 years. The photograph shows it before the science block was built in the foreground. In 1965 the school was renamed Williamwood High, and the old 'Eastwood' name was transferred to a newly built school at Capelrig Road, Newton Mearns. One wartime pupil remembers 'digging for victory' on the high playground and playing badminton with teachers when firewatching during the war. On one snowy day in 1937, an entire class of boys was belted by headmaster Mr Tait for throwing snowballs. Once a week classes had to walk a mile to Overlee Playing Fields to play sports or run cross country. In August 2006 the school was abandoned in favour of a newly built Williamwood High on Eaglesham Road at Newford. The old school has been demolished and new houses built on the site.

Clarkston Toll in the 1890s, looking south up Busby Road. The station goods yard is behind the wall on the left. Before the railway arrived the road from Netherlee crossed the area of the present car park below Clarkston Library and met the crossroads with the Old Mearns Road. In 1865 the Busby railway cut through the road from Netherlee, moving it north to the present bridge over the railway, and some of the old houses were demolished.

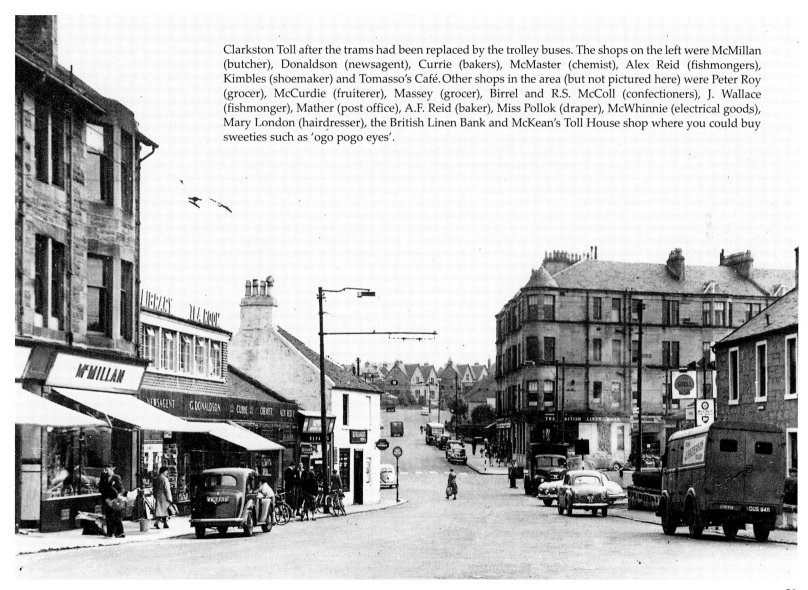

Clarkston Toll after the trams had been replaced by the trolley buses. The shops on the left were McMillan (butcher), Donaldson (newsagent), Currie (bakers), McMaster (chemist), Alex Reid (fishmongers), Kimbles (shoemaker) and Tomasso's Café. Other shops in the area (but not pictured here) were Peter Roy (grocer), McCurdie (fruiterer), Massey (grocer), Birrel and R.S. McColl (confectioners), J. Wallace (fishmonger), Mather (post office), A.F. Reid (baker), Miss Pollok (draper), McWhinnie (electrical goods), Mary London (hairdresser), the British Linen Bank and McKean's Toll House shop where you could buy sweeties such as 'ogo pogo eyes'.

On the afternoon of 21 October 1971 a major catastrophe struck Clarkston when a gas explosion blew out the front of ten shops on the ground level, causing the roof – which supported a car park – to collapse. Some cars fell through the shops to their basements. Twenty-two people tragically died, some in the shops and some in a double-decker bus that was parked outside. The shops damaged were John Menzies, Malcolm Campbell, Hamish Robertson, City Bakeries, Radio Rentals, J. & R. Milligrew, Dalziel's Furnishers, James Allan & Sons and Crown Wallpapers. In time the shops were rebuilt and the car park reopened.

Clarkston Toll in the 1980s after a particularly heavy fall of snow. The price of petrol would be attractive to many today! The Toll shops on the left replaced those destroyed in the Clarkston Disaster.

Clarkston Toll looking down Busby Road in the mid to late nineteenth century. The hamlet started in the 1790s when John Clark bought a plot at the toll and built a house and stables. In 1801 estate owner Maxwell of Williamwood advertised the toll as the site of a new village. It grew slowly, initially thanks to industry at Netherlee, then with the arrival of the railway. The houses on the right sit on the road to Netherlee, before it was cut off by the railway.

Mr Shedden's hardware shop was set back just beyond the Co-op on Busby Road and is now a charity shop. It closed when one of Mr Shedden's successors, Mr Gray, retired a few years ago. It stocked a great variety of goods and was much handier than B&Q if you ran short of nails or washers!

The top of Busby Road, Clarkston, in the early 1930s. The stationmaster's house is on the left. One of the white houses on the right belonged to Tom Lindsay, a local portrait photographer who travelled about on his bicycle. Further up the hill on the right was Arundel private school which was built of corrugated-iron sheeting and known as the 'Tin Academy'. The large house on the right, 'Midholm', was at one time home of Dr Russell, a popular and highly respected local doctor, and now forms the premises of a jeweller and a solicitors' firm.

Pupils of Arundel School, 1929. Behind is Carolside Farm which was off Hillview Drive. A Miss Cumming founded the school in two rooms in her house in Overlee Road during the First World War. In 1924 the metal-framed school was erected and lasted through the 1930s. Miss Cumming was a strict disciplinarian. She wore a coat and hat in the class, which was necessary in winter as the poorly insulated building only had coke-burning stoves in the centre of each classroom. Slates and slate pencils were used in place of paper and pencil. After the school closed it became the Labour Party Hall until it was demolished in 1941 to make way for shops.

In 1858 James Crum proposed a new railway passing through Williamwood to terminate at the printworks at Busby. Various routes were considered before the Busby railway via Clarkston was opened in 1866. Clarkston Station, shown here, quickly contributed to the growth of the area. This photograph, taken in the early 1930s, displays an advert for McTaggart and Mickel's houses at Carolside Park. The station had a small goods yard on the left and a larger mineral yard on the right, originally developed to serve Netherlee Printworks. The tracks were lifted in the 1960s to form the present car park fronting Clarkston Hall. The station had an extra entrance for train passengers from Stamperland Hill at the end of the pedestrian bridge, which was removed in the 1970s.

King George arriving at Muirend Station during the First World War for a visit to Weir's works at Cathcart. Muirend was the nearest station to Netherlee on the line to Neilston which opened in 1903. At one time it was proposed to build a Netherlee 'halt' on this line, at the bottom of Williamwood Drive. Additional Netherlee lines were planned but never built. A railway from Glasgow to Kilmarnock, via Netherlee and Mearns, would have cut Netherlee in two, and was started in 1865 but abandoned. The original proposal for the Cathcart Circle in the 1880s included a branch line to Carmunnock via Muirend and Netherlee, but this was also never built.

Clarkston Railway Station staff around 1920, when the Busby Railway was operated by the Caledonian Railway. As the railway was first intended mainly for goods traffic, the original station building was much smaller, similar to the surviving buildings at Busby and Thorntonhall. It was situated further down the line beside the road bridge and latterly housed railway staff until it was demolished in the 1970s.

A three-horse coach at Clarkston Station. The railway station served a much wider area, including Eaglesham and Mearns, and these coaches provided essential links. This is the Eaglesham coach, owned by Thomas Watt of Eaglesham's Eglinton Arms.

An Overlee Cricket Club team, sometime before the First World War. The club presumably played on Overlee farmland before Overlee Park was formed. Some of the members include: Adam McKechnie (back row, with the pipe), James Hawthorn (back row, at the right end), Neil Hawthorn (middle row, at the left end) and David Carslaw (middle row, at the right end). Overlee was a originally a small estate and when the railway cut its farmland in half in the 1860s the section at Sheddens was released for housing development. The other half continued to be farmed until becoming Overlee Park in the mid 1930s. The park was funded by the King George's Fields Foundation which was responsible for nearly 500 playing fields in the UK. In the early nineteenth century the farm steading was moved east to its present site and when foundations were dug for it, an early village was unearthed. Alleged to rival Skara Brae, it was unfortunately not preserved.

Golf Road, Clarkston, in 1948. The name of the road originates from Williamwood Golf Course which at one time also covered this area south of Eastwoodmains Road, including the site of Eastwood School. The clubhouse (Radleigh House) stood on the corner of this road and members accessed the course by crossing Eastwoodmains Road and going under a red brick bridge to reach the first tee, now the sixteenth hole. The bridge still survives, hidden behind Drumby Crescent. Williamwood Golf Course celebrated its centenary in 2006.

St Joseph's School in Sheddens opened in 1880 and moved to a new building at Oliphant Crescent, Busby, in 1964. This shows a pantomime at the school, featuring well-known Scottish comedian Larry Marshall (third left in the back row). Others include Eddie Pollock (back row, right end), Tommy Houliham (second row, first left) and, Kathleen Brady (first row, fifth from left).

The name 'Sheddens' indicates a parting of roads, and the parting in question is here at the junction of the Busby and Eaglesham roads. The Buck's Head Café was very popular, but it was later demolished to make way for the present shops. Note the Daily Record headline 'Atlantic Flight', which probably refers to Lindbergh's solo flight from New York to Paris in May 1927, the year this photograph was taken.

Harvesting hay on Cartsbridge Farm, *c.* 1926. The farm was at the top of Mansfield Road and survived until the 1960s, although it was latterly hemmed in by housing. The farm's land stretched over the hill (Cartsbridge Road) to include parts of Busby village, reaching as far as the River Cart.

The Sheddens area, looking east over the junction of Greenwood Road and Eaglesham Road, in 1927. Busby Railway viaduct is in the far right beyond George Wright's joiners shop, seen before the shops were built. In the centre only a few of the bungalows in Victoria Crescent had then been built. On the right horizon is the village of Carmunnock.

Greenbank Church was built in 1884 on the lands of Cartsbridge Farm. It was named after Greenbank Estate which purchased the farm in 1875, then gifted the land for the church. The original church in Clarkston was a mission and Sunday school held at Clarkston Toll and run by Cathcart Church. In 1888 this was taken over by Greenbank and soon merged into the new church.